103 Monkeys

Written by Harris Tobias
Illustrated by Dubbo

103 Monkeys

&
OTHER POEMS FOR CHILDREN

103 Monkeys
Copyright 2017
Casita Press
Charlottesville Virginia
ISBN: 978-1-943314-22-5

To our precious children, grand-
children and the young at heart
who treasure the music of a jolly
poem.

A Hundred Below

Put on your mittens
It's freezing out there
It feels like a hundred below
Wrap yourself up in your warm woolly down
And then you can play in the snow
Make a snow angel
And slide down the hill
Throw snowballs until you get cold
Build a snowman, make a snow fort
Better play now before you get old
Before you turn into the adult who
Warns
"Don't stick your tongue on the pole,
Kid
Don't stick your tongue on the pole."

Mealtime Friend

I used to have a monkey
I named my monkey Joel
And every morning Joel would come
And eat the corn flakes in my bowl
Monkeys don't eat corn flakes
I would tell Joel in a huff
But he would shove those corn flakes in
Until he'd had enough

At lunch time Joel would come
And sit beside my chair
He'd bang upon my lunch box
To see what was in there

He'd beg for bits of cookie
And other lunchy stuff
Until there wasn't any left
Or he'd had enough

At supper Joel would always
Sit upon my lap
He'd watch me eat my supper
And beg for any scrap
He'd help me eat my vegetables
Which I think is only fair
So I can have some chocolate cake
But that I do not share.

Some People

Some people like to watch TV
Some people like to take hikes
Some people jog in their sneakers
Some people peddle their bikes
I'm happy that everyone's different
Like snowflakes, no two are alike.

Some people ride in their autos
Some people like to take trains
Some people love when it's sunny
Some people love when it rains
How sad it would be
If all we could see
Was everyone exactly the same

The world needs all kinds of people

Just like flowers in a bouquet
We all can learn from each other
We all have something to say

Some people like to eat burgers
Some people like to eat grains
Some people are always happy
Some people always complain
How dull it would be
If you were like me
And we were all exactly the same

The world needs all kinds of people
Just like flowers in a bouquet
We all can learn from each other
We all have something to say

The Adventurer

I like to race around the Sun
And Swing upon the Moon
I climb the stars
Like monkey bars
Then fly back to my room

I don't know what will happen
Or what the day will bring
But I can see
It's bound to be
Filled with happy things

I don't know what school is like
It will be something new
But in the end
I'll take a friend
On an adventure too

I'm a brave explorer
I've been under the sea
And I've seen things
Like fish with wings
And dolphins drinking tea

I like chasing dinosaurs
For that I travel far
And flying things
With colored wings
I keep inside a jar

Another trip around the world
Then home again for tea
Life is fun
When you are an
Explorer just like me

But I'm always there for dinner
To eat my jam and bread
I'm filled with tales
Of dancing whales
You laugh at things I said

You'll marvel at my bravery
And praise the things I said
Then with a laugh
Give me a bath
And tuck me into bed

A Love Story

A giraffe and a hippo fell madly in love
The hippo was short, the giraffe towered above

They were married one day by a passing crow
And now they are man and wife don't you know

"I love you dear hippo," the tall giraffe said
And bent down to kiss her on top of her head

He bent down so low he got dizzy and fell
Which caused Mrs. Hippo to let out a yell,

"Are you alright Mr. Giraffe?"
"I'm fine," he said and they had a good laugh

Wherever they went all the beasts would declare
"My aren't you an unusual pair?"

Head Cold

I'm lying in bed with a horrible cold
My head is so stuffed it just might explode
My mother has fed me so much chicken soup
I might as well live with the hens in the coop
I'm achy and feverish and sound like a duck
And tomorrow's no school, how's that for luck?
Outside it's Spring. I can hear children calling
And I'm stuck in here, it's totally appalling
Too bad it's sunny and warm, I complain
The least it should be chilly and rain
I hate lying here with nothing to do
I'd much rather run and have fun in the sun
Wouldn't you?

Stinky Toes

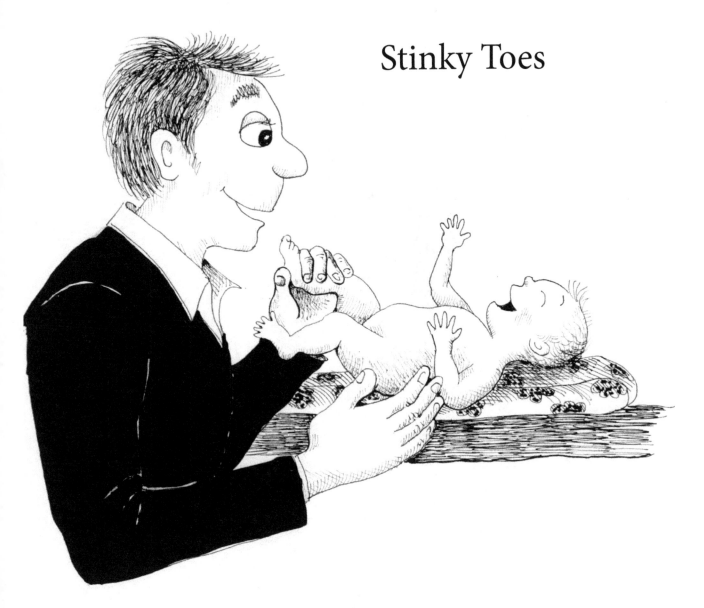

What's that smell?
I can tell.
Someone has stinky toes?
Whose toes?
Who knows?
Who has stinky toes?
I'll use my nose
Here goes
Sniff. Sniff. Sniff.

I got a whiff
Of something stinky
Little pinky toes
Wiggly piggy toes
Funny bunny toes
Teeny tiny toes.
Who has stinky toes?
Who knows?

Getting Happy

What does a giraffe do for a laugh
When he's feeling sad and alone?
He puts half and half
In his decaf
And plays a game on his phone

What's a gnu do
When the work day is through
And his mood is in need of a boost?
He does arabesques
At a few discotheques
And finds his spirits jazzy and juiced

When a dog's feeling down
He slips out of town
And gives a good howl at the moon
After a howl
He goes on a prowl
And sleeps til the next afternoon

My Dog's Nose

I Have a dog with a twitchy nose
Back and forth his black nose goes
Sometimes it goes left to right
And sometimes it goes up and down
But whichever way it goes
My dog has a twitchy nose.

I Saw The Sea

As I walked along the shore
The sea saw me
And the sea I saw
The sea saw me and I saw the sea
Oh the sea saw me and the sea I saw
As I walked along the shore
The sea saw me and I saw the sea

When the sea saw me
It gave a wave
And so a wave
To the sea I gave
The sea gave me a little wave
And a wave to the sea I gave
When the sea saw me and I saw the sea

As I walked along the sand
The sea it took my little hand
My hand is small and the sea is grand
Still it shook my little hand
As I walked along the strand
Me and the sea, the sea and me

The sea was blue
And the sky was too
And the seabirds cried ta-wit ta-woo
When I saw the sea and the sea saw me
Oh the sea was blue and the seabirds cried
And I felt so warm inside
When I saw the sea and the sea saw me

Zombie Child

My mother and father were zombies
I guess that makes me a zombie as well
At least I think I'm a zombie
Sometimes it's so hard to tell

Sometimes I think that my family
Is different than others in town
Each night after dark
We go to the park
And stiffly waddle around

Each night when I come home for dinner
It's always the very same thing
A big plate of brains and a salad
Mom thinks highly of greens

At school I bring my own sandwich
Mother wants me to eat lots of grains
So I lather on peanut butter
Then a layer of jelly and brains

Sometimes I think that my family
Is different than others in town
Each night after dark
We go to the park
And stiffly waddle around

At school people think that I'm lazy
Cause I don't like to play silly games
They laugh and play tag
While I reach in my bag
And nibble away on fried brains

Sometimes I think that my family
Is different than others in town
Each night after dark
We go to the park
And stiffly waddle around

Little Muffin

Little Muffin
Little Muffin
Don't run away.
Don't worry Mommy
I'll be back someday

Little Muffin
Little Muffin
Where did you go?
I went to Grandma's
To learn how to sew

Little Muffin
Little Muffin
Why are you sad?
Because I can't find
My dear Mom and Dad

Little Muffin
Little Muffin
How old are you?
I'm five years old
And my sister is two

Little Muffin
Little Muffin

Why do you smile?
Because I am going
To play for a while

Little Muffin
Little Muffin
Where do you run?
I ran to Grandpa's
And had lots of fun

Little Muffin
Little Muffin
Why do you laugh?
Because Daddy said
I am taking a bath

Little Muffin
Little Muffin
What's that you said?
I'm tired and sleepy
And going to bed

Little Muffin
Little Muffin
Did I hear you speak?
I didn't hear anything
She's fast asleep

Big Appetites

When I was thin
My waist curved in
And people admired my figure
Now I am stout
And my waist curves out
Leaving no doubt I am bigger

When I was young
I commanded my tongue
And told it enough was enough
But now as you see
My tongue commands me
And is constantly calling my bluff

The result is quite clear
I'm shaped like a sphere
And I no longer care how it feels
While my shape anatomical
Might strike you as comical
It doesn't interfere with my meals

Some people I find
Can attain peace of mind
From hiking and biking and such
But for people like me
Life's true ecstasy
Comes only from eating too much

Fight Night

It was billed as the biggest fight of the year
Nothing even came close
On one side was Samson, the fierce Polar Bear,
On the other was Irving, the mouse

The referee was Fido, the dog,
A ref considered both fair and clean
He'd been reffing prize fights for so long
There was nothing that he hadn't seen

The crowd was truly enormous that night
They were packed tight around the ring
Everyone knew this would be quite a fight
And they wanted to see everything

The crowd grew wild when Samson appeared
Everyone expected the big bear would win
When Irving entered they booed and they jeered
Anxious for the fight to begin

Samson, the bear, was as strong as an ox
He had never lost even one fight
While Irving, the mouse, could hardly box
No one expected much of a fight

Fido, the ref, told them to fight fair
Using Marquis of Queensbury rules
No kicking, no biting, and no pulling hair
No cheating or acting like fools

The odds on the mouse were two thousand to one
How could a mouse beat a bear?
Before anyone knew it the fight had begun
You could taste excitement in the air

Right from the start things began to go wrong
It was plain that the bear was in trouble
Irving, the mouse, proved surprisingly strong
And his speed was far more than double

The mouse was surprisingly quick on his feet
And zipped back and forth at a run
After three minutes the bear was dizzy and beat
He was saved when the bell ended round one

In his corner the bear tried to regain his poise
His trainer dried him and gave him a drink

You could hardly hear the bell over the noise
The fight resumed but not how you'd think

Round two started off much the same
With Samson landing no blows
The crowd was calling out Samson's shame
When the mouse jumped on the bear's nose

Samson stared at the mouse on his face
And saw his chance to give it a whack
He connected so hard he teetered in place
Then he staggered and fell on his back

Fido, the ref, counted slowly to ten
But Samson had knocked himself out
The little mouse had somehow managed to win
Beyond any shadow of doubt

That was the fight twixt the mouse and the bear
And I realize how strange it sounds
Irving won the fight fair and square
And did it in less than two rounds

Tangles

How is it that when I go to sleep
My hair is brushed and combed and neat
But when I wake up and leave my bed
Something's happened to my head?
My hair's a knotted, tangled mess
It can't be combed and I confess
It would take a team of docs
To undo even half my knots
The reason is quite plain to me,
There's only one thing it can be,
Something visited while I slept
Something into my bedroom crept
And using all its furry paws
Ran my hair through sticky jaws
And spread something gooey on my locks
And turned my hair to tangley knots
It's the only thing that can explain
Why I go through so much pain
In the morning when I dare
To try and comb my tangled hair
The Tangle Monster visited me
I don't know what else it could it be?

Tummy Ache

Tummy ache, tummy ache
Too much onion and baloney cake
Too much pudding with spaghetti flakes
Too many chocolate and pizza shakes

I know, I know, I should have stopped
With a bowl of soup and slice of pie
Topped with ice cream, pickles and my oh my
But my tongue was so happy It wanted more
Pancakes, cereal the whole darn store

Now I'm sorry and my tummy aches
No more onion and baloney cakes
No more pudding with spaghetti flakes
And no more chocolate and pizza shakes
Next time I'll go to the store alone
And leave my tummy and my tongue at home

Tea For Two

I never saw a dinosaur
I don't suppose I ever will
But if I saw one walk down the street
It sure would be a thrill
"Hello," I'd say. "How are you today?
Would you like a bite to eat?"
The dinosaur would give a roar
And he would take his seat
Then we'd sit and sip a cup of tea
And speak of many things
I never saw a dinosaur before
But think that's how it would be

103 Monkeys

A family of monkeys lived in a tree
I think they numbered one hundred and three
That's too many monkeys, too many for me
One hundred and three is a goodly amount
One hundred and three is too many to count
They chitter and chatter and make so much noise
I cant think, can't sleep I am losing my poise
I'm hoping they will just move away
But something tells me they're here to stay
I'm almost afraid to go outside to play
There are too many monkeys I think you'll agree
Too many monkeys up in that tree
How many are there? One hundred and three

Bad Dogs Get No Chicken

Bad dog
Down
Now what you gonna do
Bad dog
Down
No chicken for you

I told you get down doggy
And what did you do
You jumped up on the sofa
No chicken for you

When the mailman came you barked and growled
No chicken for you
When the moon came out you sat and howled
No chicken for you

Bad dogs get no chicken
If they don't mend their wicked ways
Bad dogs gonna eat kibble
For the rest of their days

I warned you once
I warned you twice
You're lucky to get beans and rice
Cause bad dogs get no chicken
So heed me and be nice

On the Road to Bimbombey

On the road to Bimbombey
I met a man along the way
One eye was blue and one was gray
He reminded me of a cloudy day

On the road to Bimbombey
I saw a man with a white toupee
He smiled at me with teeth of clay
I got scared and I ran away

On the road to Bimbombey
The merchant's wares are on display
A nickle each for a fine parfait
I bought a tart from a silver tray

On the road to Bimbombey
I saw some little girls at play
They played tag and keep away
Their motions made a fine ballet

On the road to Bimbombey
The sun was beating at midday
I saw some piles of golden hay
And that is where my head I lay

When I awoke the sky was gray
My hair and clothes in disarray
I looked a sight that much I'll say
On the road to Bimbombey

Barefoot

Let your feet go free
Let your feet go free
Oh to feel the Earth beneath your feet
To feel the grass and feel the street
Just let your toes go without their clothes

Let your feet go free
Let your feet go free
It's such a footsy world you'll see
If you just let them be
Let your feet go free

Oh Mr. Business man in your business suit
Wouldn't you look cute if you freed your feet?
Just take off your shoes and socks
Feel the pebbles, feel the rocks
Practice nudity below the knee

Let your feet go free
Let your feet go free
Think of all the friends your toes will meet
If you just free your feet
Let your feet go free
Let your feet go free

Doing Chores

My mother said "Go make your bed.
"Make your bed," she roars
I made my bed just like she said
I hate doing chores
After breakfast mama pointed to the sink
She wanted me to put my dishes there
At least that's what I think
She made me pick up all my toys
Before I went outdoors
Did I mention how much
I hate doing chores?
Later on my mother cried
"Pick your clothes up off the floors."
Just 'cause I was in the closet
Doesn't mean I was trying to hide
"Clean your room,"
I heard her boom
Not something one ignores
Straightening up and cleaning
Are two things I deplores
Did I mention just how much
I hate doing chores?

At The Robot Zoo

I went to the robot zoo
I wanted to see what the animals do
When no one was looking

So I hid in the dark
Til they closed up the park
And I had the most marvelous view
And I saw what was cooking

I saw them feed the chimpanzees
On motor oil and batteries

The kangaroo wiggled his metal ears
When they tossed him a salad of wires and gears

I saw them remove the zebra's stripes
They rubbed them off with Handy Wipes

The robot monkey didn't swing
In fact he didn't do a thing
I watched them use a pair of pliers
To replace his monkey wires

The robot bear didn't go anywhere
He just sat around with a vacant stare
They opened him up looking for clues
Finally replacing a burnt out fuse

The sleek black panther looked fantastic
His coat was made of shiny plastic
They wiped him down with an oily rag
And fed him something from a paper bag

The robot giraffe gave me a laugh
They used metal polish to give him a bath

The robot snake looked totally fake
He could hardly keep himself awake
A couple of guys got a big surprise
When he hissed and opened his eyes

The old ant eater couldn't be sweeter
I saw him lick the old zookeeper
The old zookeeper did a funny dance
His pants were filled with robot ants

The iron horse gave his head a toss
He showed his keepers who was boss
A noble beast, to say the least,
As sleek and smooth as apple sauce

The robot lion opened his jaw
And let out a funny roar
It rattled the bars and shook the ground
But had a most unnatural sound

What I thought was a heap of scrap
Was really an elephant taking a nap
I could swear it was a pile of junk
Until it offered me its trunk

All in all, I was happy to see
That the robot animals were just like me

Twenty two Tiny Turtles

22 tiny turtles climbed out of the sand
21 tiny turtles thought life was grand
20 tiny turtles smiled at a joke
19 tiny turtles went for a soak
18 tiny turtles rolled on the lawn
17 tiny turtles partied 'til dawn
16 tiny turtles laughed at a show
15 tiny turtles went for a row
14 tiny turtles sang in a choir
13 tiny turtles danced 'round a fire
12 tiny turtles swam with their mother
11 tiny turtles tickled each other
10 tiny turtles frolicked in the sea
9 tiny turtles had cookies and tea
8 tiny turtles jumped up and down
7 tiny turtles drove into town
6 tiny turtles splashed in the lake
5 tiny turtles ate ice cream and cake
4 tiny turtles got caught in the rain
3 tiny turtles rode on a train
2 tiny turtles listened to rap
1 tiny turtle went home for a nap

Cat Calls

My cat's calls are very loud
You can hear her in a crowd
I once heard someone complain
That they could hear my cat in Maine
That's how loud my cat meowed

Flying Elephants

If elephants were more like birds
They'd be so much easier to see
They'd fill the forest with their calls
And flit from tree to tree

If elephants were more like birds
I don't think I'd like their song
Screaching trumpets in the morn
Strikes the ear a bit too strong

Their nests would be enormous
And so too would be their eggs
And they'd have giant feathers
Covering their legs

One thing is certain
As you can plainly see
If elephants were more like birds
We'd need a stronger tree

My Shadow

My shadow is a sticky thing
It sticks to me like glue
And whenever I'm in the sun
My shadow is there too

Inside is another story
My shadow I can lose
If my shadow wants to play
Inside I can refuse

But outside when the sun is high
My shadow will not leave my side
I try and run away or hide
But no matter what I do
My shadow is right next to me
Attached right to my shoe
Sometimes I wish he'd go away
And find another friend
I've tried everything I know
To make him go
What would you recommend?

In the Bahamas

In the Bahamas they don't wear pajamas
They cover themselves with with a shawl
But in Bermuda, things much cruder
There they sleep in nothing at all

Folks in Milwaukee are chatty and talkie
At least that's the way that they seem
While those in Detroit are more verbally adroit
But they don't always say what they mean

The natives of Durban wrap their heads in a turban
Before going out in the sun
The sun in Australia can cause massive brain failure
And everyone knows that's no fun

Folks in Montana won't eat a banana
They prefer a less tropical taste
Bananas they feel have too slippery a peel
So most of them just go to waste

There are men in Toledo who won't wear a tuxedo
They feel they are setting a style
At a prom or a ball you won't see one at all
You'd mistake them for clothes in a pile

There are women in Maine who like to complain
That their boyfriends bore them to the bone
While they like romances and parties and dances
Their boyfriends just want to stay home

A Crooked Tale

Once there was a crooked man
Who had a crooked smile
He used a crooked walking stick
To walk a crooked mile
He came upon a crooked house
With a crooked roof and floor
He used his crooked walking stick
To knock upon the door
"Who's there?" a crooked voice
called out
From within the crooked room
It was a crooked lady
Sweeping with a crooked broom
"What do you want young man?"
 she asked
Her voice was hoarse and sore
"Why do you come a knocking
At my front door?"

"I've come to say "I love you,"
The crooked young man said
And it wasn't long thereafter
That the crooked pair were wed
They were married in a crooked
church
By a crooked priest
And on their crooked wedding day
They served a crooked feast
The crooked table groaned
With crooked plates of meats
And after, there was wedding cake
And other crooked treats
All their crooked friends were there
And all the crooked guests
Raised their crooked glasses
And wished the crooked couple
Peace and happiness

Farm Song

If you were a rooster
And I was a rooster
I know just what we'd do
We'd climb on the barn
And greet the dawn
With a cock-a-doodle-doo

cock-a-doodle-doo
cock-a-doodle-doo
We'd climb on the barn
And greet the dawn
With a cock-a-doodle-doo

If you were a milk cow
And I was a milk cow
I know just what we'd do
We'd chew on the weeds
And lie in the leaves
Singing moo, moo, moo, moo, moo

moo, moo, moo, moo, moo
moo, moo, moo, moo, moo
We'd chew on the weeds
And lie in the leaves
Singing moo, moo, moo, moo, moo

If you were a lamb
And I was a lamb
I know just what we'd do
We'd frolic and play
In the sun all day
Singing Baa, baa, baa, baa, boo

Baa, baa, baa, baa, boo
Baa, baa, baa, baa, boo
We'd frolic and play
In the sun all day
Singing Baa, baa, baa, baa, boo

If you were a pigeon
And I was a pigeon
I know just what we'd do
We'd sleep in the barn
Where it's nice and warm
Singing coo, coo, coo, coo, coo

Coo, coo, coo, coo, coo
Coo, coo, coo, coo, coo
We'd sleep in the barn
Where it's nice and warm
Singing coo, coo, coo, coo, coo

If you were a owl
And I was an owl
I know just what we'd do
We'd stay at home
Til the sun went down
Singing who, who, who, who

Who, who, who, who, who
Who, who, who, who, who
We'd stay at home
Til the sun went down
Singing who, who, who, who

The Giant's Lunch

The kitchen was busy cooking a bunch
It was late and the giant wanted his lunch
Everything had to be prepared just right
For the giant had a really huge appetite
And everyone knew when the giant was hungry
It didn't take much to make him angry
So they made sure the food was good
Down to the very last bite

The Giant sat down at the table
And tied his napkin under his chin
That napkin was as big as a bed sheet
But it looked like nothing on him
The servants started bringing the lunch in
More food that you've ever seen
There were crepes the size of a small skating rink
And a soup bowl as big as your kitchen sink
And buckets of water for him to drink
A pile of sandwiches as tall as a man
More than enough to feed your whole clan
Next came a fifty pound mushroom tart

And believe me when I tell you that was only the start
Out came an entire bar-b-qued cow
Three hens, four ducks and a goat
If anyone could eat so much, I don't know how,
But it all disappeared down his throat

Finally they wheeled out six dessert carts
Now that was something to see
Cookies and ice cream and 20 fruit tarts
Enough sweets for a hundred and three
Eclairs and cookies and a whole ice cream cake
It is hard to believe all he consumed
If you even thought of eating that much
You know that you would be doomed
That meal could have fed my town for a month
And that was only the giant's lunch

How Many

How many sea shells lie on a beach?
How many waves lap the shore?
How many hairs do you have on your head?
How many socks in your drawer?

Ten thousand sea shells lie on the beach
Ten million waves lap the shore
Ten thousand hairs grow on your head
But only ten socks in your drawer

How many fish in the ocean?
How many birds that can fly?
How many trees in the forest?
How many stars in the sky?

There are billions of fish in the ocean
There are millions of birds that can fly
There are trillions of trees in the forest
We see five thousand stars with our eye

How many drops in a rain storm?
How many leaves on a tree?
How many ants in an ant hill?
How many cells make a me?

There are billions of drops in a rain storm
There are thousands of leaves on a tree
There are ten thousand ants in an ant hill
And trillions of cells make a me

On the Bottom of the Sea

On the bottom of the sea
On the bottom of the bay
Where the starfish shine
And the mermaids play
I'll meet you there
At a quarter past nine
When the dolphins dance
And the monkfish dine

Oh the sea is wide
And the bay is deep
Watch the swordfish duel
See the marlin leap
So come with me
And we will play
On the bottom of the sea
On the bottom of the bay

We'll laugh and sing
Like a fishy thing
Just you and me
On the bottom of the sea
On the bottom of the bay
Where the starfish shine
And the mermaids play
Where the swordfish duel
And cuttlefish graze
The Earth's a jewel
Come along with me
And be amazed

Tell Us A Story Grandpa

Everyone thought that grandpa looked queer
With his big bushy beard and his white frizzy hair
But his heart was warm and his mind was clear
And he had many stories to tell
The children would gather to hear him recite
They'd huddle around him their faces alight
This was the magical time of the night
He'd place them under his spell

"Tell us a story," a grand child would ask
And Grandpa was always up to the task
He'd pause for a second and drink from his flask
His stories would take them away
He told them of princes and far away lands
Of monsters and maidens and outlaw bands
Lost in dark forests or on hot desert sands
And he always began the same way

There once was a child exactly like you
And somehow that kid would just know what to do
When the giants attacked or some bad pirate crew
Came banging on the gates
That kid would make a suggestion or two
About what he thought the grown ups should do
And of course they would listen because they just knew
That the child would change all their fates

The giant would trip and fall on its face
The pirates, defeated, would run in disgrace
And all of the monsters would leave with no trace
And the world would appear much the same
The child resumed living the life that he had
Once again safe with his mother and dad
He learned a lesson about good and bad
And was eager to face it again

Whatever bad things sought to invade
He knew his grand children would not be afraid
Those wonderful stories made them feel brave
And they never ran from a fight
They grew up knowing just what to do
No menace too great that they wouldn't come through
They all grew up fearless and noble and true
And always did what was right

Dragon Dreams

Have you ever seen a dragon
Streak across the skies
With fire in his belly
And fire in his eyes?
I don't suppose you ever will
Since dragons aren't real
But if I ever saw one
I know exactly how I'd feel
My heart would start pounding
My head would fill with dread
And I suspect you'd find me
Underneath my bed

My House Is A Zoo

What can I do?
What can I do?
It seems like my house has turned
into a zoo
There's a giraffe in my bath
Don't laugh
There's an owl in my towel
And a mink in my sink
There's a llama in my pajama
I'm calling my mamma
And if that isn't enough
Silly stuff
There's a gnu in my shoe
A goat in my coat
There's a dove with my glove
And a bat in my hat
How about that?

There are ants in my pants
And a fox in my box
A baboon's in my room
And a bear's in my chair
I don't really care but
A sloth in my broth
And a snake in my cake
Are a little too much
For a child to take
So I'm going to sleep
And when I awake
I hope that they're gone
Back to the barn
And leave all of my stuff alone
For a bug in the rug
And a whale in the mail
Is not what I want in my home.

We Love Our Cats

Cats as you know are selfish and vain
No matter how much you do they always complain
Feed me; pet me; my litter box stinks
Humans are servants that what a cat thinks
Give me attention; open the door;
I'll let you know when I need something more
Sometimes a cat will just jump in your lap
You think that she likes you but she just wants a nap
Sometimes she'll purr and say here I am
She's trying to get you to open a can
Of cat food and after she's dined
She has no further use for you or your kind
Cats can be useful and are quite ornamental
But you have to admit they are quite temperamental.

Elephant Envy

Mimi's elephant is pretty
Much prettier than mine
And he's such a nice color
And she dresses him so fine.
My elephant is very smart
Just not as smart as Ben's
My elephant can count to four
His can count to ten
My elephant is very big
But Ashley's is even bigger
My elephant is very sweet
But Frank's is so much sweeter
My elephant is strong
But Sadie's is much stronger
His ears are almost twice the size
And his trunk is longer
But you know I don't really care,
My elephant's just fine
One thing I know he's always there
I'm his and he is mine

The Hamster and the Whale

A hamster and a humpbacked whale
Set up house together
The hamster did the laundry
The whale kept his eye on the weather

It's going to rain today
Said the humpback with a sigh
If you do the wash tomorrow
It won't have a chance to dry

The hamster said "The sun is shining."
Indeed the day was bright and clear
"Besides," said the hamster
I am out of underwear."

And so he did the laundry
Though the sky was turning grey
I should have listened to you old friend
But I did the laundry anyway

When the wash was finished
And thunder began to boom
The hamster and the humpbacked whale
Hung their clothes inside their room

Tender Loving Care

The world is fragile, the world is fine
We must protect the grand design
We are stewards of the Earth
Let's learn to share

Share the sunshine, share the space
Stand up tall and state the case
Make this world a better place
Share the land and share the seas
We can't do everything we please
There's a lot of life that need our care

We are passengers on spaceship Earth
And this world deserves it's true worth
And tender loving care
Can make us all aware
Tender loving care

Let's give the animals room to roam
Let's not destroy their home
Let's leave them undisturbed
Every lion, every rhino, every bird

This world is the only one we've got
From space we're just a tiny dot
We must learn to take much better care
And start to share
With tender loving care

Some Other books by Harris Tobias that you might enjoy:

How The Cat Got Its Whiskers

The Adventures of MoonRivet

The Turtle's Ball

At The Robot Zoo

Five Little Froggies

The Adventures of Rocket Bob

The King's Dream

A Wish Too Far

The Broody Little Hen

The Big Fat Counting Book

The Three Chocolatiers

The Three Swords

The Wisdom of Yaqui the Bear

The Catch of the Day

The Contest

DragonSong

Square Sally in Circletown

How Birds Got Their Colors

The Amulet of Power

DreamShip Lullaby

A Wish Too Far

A Child's Book of Riddles

A Chanukah Story

5 Children's Poems

A Prisoner of Beauty

The Stone Apples

Baker's Dozen

Bug Alphabet

Catch of the Day

Farm Song

Stinky Feet

How The Pelican Got Its Beak

How The Zebra Got Its Stripes

A Child's Book of Riddles

Snails, Scales & Animal Tales

Storyland Jack

The Three Brothers

Trumpet The Homeless Troll

And for older readers:

A Felony of Birds

The Greer Agency

Alien Fruit

Chronon, Time Travel Stories

Hold The Anchovies

Peaceful Intent

The Stang

Dick Danks, The Collected Stories

Assisted

All titles are available on

Amazon in print and as ebooks..

Just enter Harris Tobias in the search field.

CPSIA information can be obtained
at www.ICGtesting.com
Printed in the USA
BVHW09*2321030818
523231BV00006B/43/P